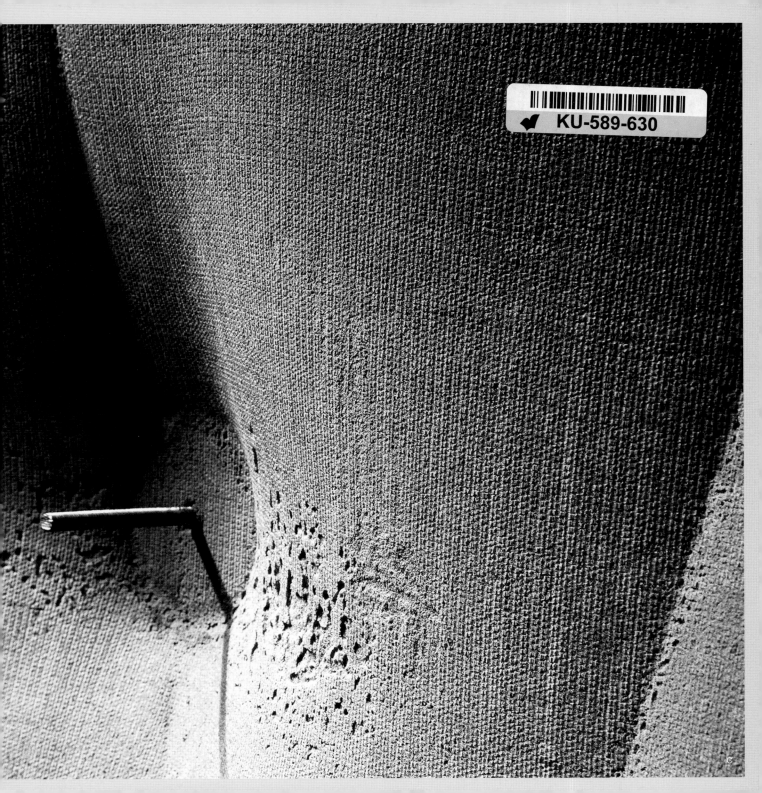

ACKNOWLEDGEMENTS

The Concrete Centre wishes to thank all the speakers for their contribution to the success of the 2005 series, for helping with the supply of images and for assisting with notes for the drafting of this text.

For information on future 'Concrete Elegance' events, please contact The Concrete Centre or The Building Centre Trust. See inside the back cover for details.

Written and edited by
David Bennett,
David Bennett Associates

Booklet designed by
Kneath Associates

Copyright permission and photo credits are as follows:
Park Lane – Rolfe Judd Architecture/Trent Concrete; Lincoln Museum – Panter Hudspith Architects/Hugh Strange; Hoop Lane – Tito Chaudhuri/David Bennett; Jackson Lane – Steve Bowkett/David Bennett; Fabric Concrete Wall – Dirk Lellau; Saterinrinne Housing Development – Jussi Tiainen/Brunow and Maunula Architects; SID Building – 3XNielson Architects; Rene Coty Avenue – Christian Hauvette Architects; Katson Building – White Architects/Åke E:son Lindman and Natasja Jovic

Thanks to Birkhäuser – Publishers for Architecture for granting permission to use short edited summaries of text derived from *The Art of Precast Concrete* for the following projects: Park Lane, Saterinrinne Housing Development, SID Building, Rene Coty Avenue and Katson Building.

© The Concrete Centre 2006

Published by
RIBA Publishing
15 Bonhill Street
London EC2P 4EA

ISBN-10 1 85946 239 1
ISBN-13 978 1 85946 239 3

Stock Code 58498

RIBA Publishing is part of RIBA Enterprises Ltd
www.ribaenterprises.com

CONTENTS

CONCRETE ELEGANCE IS A SERIES OF ARCHITECTURAL PRESENTATIONS GIVEN AT THE BUILDING CENTRE BY LEADING DESIGNERS, INNOVATORS AND MANUFACTURERS OF CONCRETE.

E

CONCRETE ELEGANCE//
01OVERVIEW

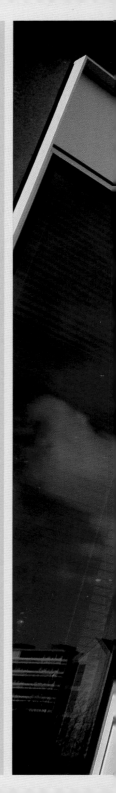

OVERVIEW

The possibilities and scope for concrete in all its forms continues to evolve and surprise – whether it's pink, purple, poured, polished, prefabricated, pulverised or sandwiched, the material's ageless character seems to burst with new ideas and innovations. The projects highlighted in this booklet are no exception to this trend, yet there are a few mature, tried and tested ideas that remain strangely dormant in the consciousness of some designers. Thanks to the first presentation in this series, we have been given a timely wake-up call.

Precast concrete has not found many admirers amongst young architects in the UK – the 'word on the street' is that it is perceived as labour intensive, heavy and expensive. This may be so for refurbishment work, where it has to match the context of adjoining monumental stone-clad buildings in city-centre locations. But that is not the case for new-build, where there are other significant, lightweight, lean, fast-build options that we seem to be ignoring while the fastidious Finns, the daring Danes, the seductive Swedes and the fashionable French – along with their pragmatic contractors – embrace them with gusto. So it is a source of

some delight to hear that there are a number of precast companies that can offer GRC (glassfibre reinforced concrete) cladding panels in the UK, and one or two well-established home-grown architects who have specified this material and like it. GRC is considerably lighter in self weight than conventional precast, yet it has the same surface appearance and can be moulded into complex curving profiles and large panellised units. On a major building at 25–35 Park Lane, London it has been cast as slender pilaster columns and cantilever fascia units that encase the bay windows and façade. The quality of the surface finish was so good that the architects, Rolfe Judd, thought the actual Portland stone panels looked dull and drab by comparison. The 20mm-thick units were so lightweight that they could be installed as part of the curtain-wall package, using cradles rather than heavy cranage.

Continuing on the theme of modern precast, the second half of the lecture series focused on precast architecture in Northern Europe and coincided with the launch of a new book, *The Art of Precast Concrete* published by Birkhäuser and sponsored by The Concrete Centre. The four projects presented

in this review are much-curtailed summaries of the detailed descriptions and explanations to be found in the book, to which the interested reader is recommended for further information. What has emerged from the talks is the revelation that precast is the dominant form of concrete construction in Scandinavia because it is the cheapest way to build. Architects and structural engineers specify and detail precast buildings working strictly to the manufacturer's standard units; the contractor builds the precast structure and takes delivery of the precast components, while the manufacturer simply makes the units. It is a logical process, and this explains why it is so competitively priced. In Finland, for example, we were informed that precast sandwich-panel construction is the preferred building method for over 80 per cent of all residential buildings, a trend which is similar for both Sweden and Denmark. What about the resulting architecture: is it bland, repetitive and boring? Hardly – good architecture is about good design, rather than expensive materials, and that truism is exemplified in the Saterinrinne Housing Project in Helsinki and the SID office building in Arhus, both of which exploit sandwich-panel construction. Linda Mattsson of

White Architects in Stockholm made a compelling argument for specifying standard grey precast components – beams, double-T floor units, columns, staircases and core walls – transforming them into the finished architecture of a taut, open-plan office building of impressive scale and visual impact. Christian Hauvette of Christian Hauvette Architects, on the other hand, showed great dexterity, rigour and skill in the detailing and fabrication of a totally bespoke precast structure for a speculative office building in Paris, in order to express the architecture without decoration or adornment. It would be difficult to find many buildings of this quality, at such low cost, in the UK.

The second event in the series was a lecture on the Lincoln City and County Museum, designed by architects Panter Hudspith. This building constitutes a major step forward for in situ concrete finishes, and, on seeing the finish first-hand, it is obvious that the quality of the board-marked surface in the café area is every bit as good as it appears in the photographs, and is as smooth as porcelain. A great deal has been said about self-compacting concrete, with claims about 'no labour costs' and big savings in construction time, but I have yet to find a contractor who will do it for the same money as conventional compacted concrete! It does cost more, as we heard from Lafarge Ready Mixed Concrete; it does need careful and constant monitoring of the sand grading and the coarse aggregate in order to get it right. But when you see the results and the ability of the material to flow into awkward geometric shapes it is well worth the expense. Here is a poured-in-place material that can produce finishes and formed shapes which were only thought feasible with precast concrete. The added value is that it can be built as a monolithic load-carrying structure with built-in thermal mass.

Recycling, reducing waste and cutting carbon emissions has been discussed and deliberated in the architectural press and technical journals so frequently that we can nowadays become rather complacent about it. BBC News recently reported that scientist Dr Jonathan Gregory of Reading University believes that the ice cap over Greenland could melt completely and irreversibly by 2350, due to a continuing global temperature rise of 3°C. He suggests that there has already been a small, barely perceptible, rise in sea level due to this ice melt, and the predictions are that in a 1000 years' time sea levels could rise by as much as 2.1m (7 feet). What can we do to help right now? The third presentation in the series suggested some small but significant

ways in which we can help the environment. Tito Chaudhuri explained how the birch-ply formwork used for casting the exposed concrete walls of his house extension was recycled as the external cladding. That formwork would otherwise have been disposed of, creating methane which is a worse global polluter than carbon emissions. This idea can be extended to the selection of formwork for reuse as partitions, flooring and interior panels as well as exterior cladding. Much of our waste glass is recycled to make bottles and goblets, some formed into marbles for the food industry and some processed and graded as decorative aggregates for landscaping. However, up to now none has been used to make building products – such as, for example, glass-aggregate terrazzo. Steve Bowkett showed us how he and a local builder made an in situ concrete worktop for his new kitchen using recycled crushed glass fines salvaged from TV monitor screens and terrazzo-type aggregates made from 3–5mm crushed green glass bottles. With white cement bought from a local builder's merchant as the binder, the concrete matrix of waste glass and cement has produced a very attractive, hard-wearing worktop from recycled waste material. Alan Chandler, in his presentation, described a new way of forming concrete using geotextile membranes very like the material we might use as a weed suppressor under pathways. The free-form shape and duvet-like protrusions of the concrete follow the contours of the pressure gradient acting on the fabric textile. It is a new art form based on the pioneering work of Mark West. What emerges from this technology is the elimination of traditional 18mm-thick ply formwork and its replacement with a synthetic membrane 1mm thick supported by a light framework that uses less material resources – another good idea to help the environment.

Why not make a resolution and personal commitment to reduce waste, design more energy-efficient buildings and help clean up our own patch of the planet? Why not try concrete which is 100% recyclable!

David Bennett
June, 2006.

CONCRETE ELEGANCE//
02GLASSFIBRE REINFORCED
CONCRETE (GRC)

Glassfibre Reinforced Concrete (GRC)
a modern lightweight cladding
Graham Fairley, Rolfe Judd Architects and
David Walker, Trent Concrete Ltd

This versatile and durable product is fast becoming fashionable on commercial and residential projects worldwide. It's the lightweight high-tech concrete cladding alternative that comes with no load penalty or heavy cranage requirements.

25–35 Park Lane, London
Graham Fairley, Rolfe Judd Architecture

The office development is formed around a new landscaped square, creating an attractive public open space and a tranquil approach to the main entrance from Curzon Street. It was built to a conceptual design by Michael Hopkins that has been reinterpreted and detailed by Rolfe Judd Architecture. The building offers 7,615 sq m of prestigious office accommodation with unrivalled views of Hyde Park.

The external envelope is an aluminium framing system supporting Portland stone ashlar spandrels, double-glazed bay windows, lightweight GRC-column pilasters and GRC 'bird's mouth' reveals below the bay windows. Stainless-steel brackets support the non-structural aluminium wind posts that run up the corners of the bay windows. At the upper floor levels there are brises-soliel that overhang the façade and form a continuous balcony with a guard rail.

Our brief was to work to the original concept design and revise the way the details worked so that the build cost would be not more than £17m. That is considerably less than the budget for the Hopkins original – the pound notes were in the façade. In essence, we had to halve the façade cost without changing its appearance. The Portland stone, the

precast columns and the cast aluminium had to remain, but instead of designing the assembly as load-bearing with solid precast elements we designed the elevation as cladding, as a skin that was structurally redundant. By doing so, the façade became much simpler and faster to erect. In the original scheme the façade had to be built with the floors in the construction cycle and this impacted hugely on the programme time. Now, we could build the structure and bolt on the cladding afterwards.

One of our first ideas was to make the solid precast columns from lightweight GRC column shells, which drastically cut the down the dead weight while retaining the monumental appearance. The bay window trims and pilaster columns were designed as 20mm-thick GRC units which would fit onto the curtain walling frame and be erected by the curtain walling contractor. The storey-high cladding units with the feature bay windows were designed as pods with a metal floor and steel edge beams that bolted to the structural floor. Each pod had an aluminium 'roof' with an aluminium trim that connected to the floor above. The glazing, GRC spandrel and pilaster column units, and the flat Portland ashlar all had to be fitted to the cladding frame. GRC is a good architectural product but the organisations that promote it on their websites or

through sales literature do it a great disservice by trivialising it as a fanciful cheap product suitable for bird baths, Corinthian columns, hideous statues, Greek urns and artificial rocks for theme parks. It gives the wrong messages and connotations to the architectural profession. We prefer to call it 'lightweight precast precast' for obvious reasons.

Trent Concrete won the GRC supply contract and Plus Wall, the whole cladding package. I could not say whether the GRC price was cheaper than normal precast precast, but it was competitive for our project. We resolved the supply and installation of the cladding elements by having Plus Wall erect the whole system and Trent deliver the units for Plus Wall to fit on site. The GRC was colour-matched to the Portland 'Grove Whitbed' ashlar supplied by Albion Stone, and in many ways it was superior. We detailed the fascias to ensure that water was dispersed away from the panels and ashlar to minimise dirt staining. Where we have rain running on to the GRC spandrel panel from the glazing above it, we have sloped the panels inwards from top to bottom and introduced a small drip detail. There is metal backing to the panel, which acts as an effective water barrier and protection to the insulation.

GRC Construction

David Walker, Trent Concrete Ltd

GRC is composed of a mortar mix of cement, selected crushed aggregates, sand, fillers, admixtures and water, and alkali-resistant glassfibre strands. The glassfibre is typically 38–51mm long and 10 to 30 microns in diameter. It obtains its alkali resistance from a coating applied over the glass strands in the manufacturing process.

For high quality architectural cladding applications, a face coat of 4mm is sprayed into the mould and rolled to remove any voids before the backing-coat mix of glassfibre filaments and mortar is applied. The face mix is typically a blend of white cement, pigment and crushed rock fines with a maximum aggregate size of 3mm. The mortar mix for the face and backing coats should ideally have a sand: cement ratio of 1:1 or, better still, 2:1 to reduce reversible shrinkage movement in service. The backing mix is standard grey cement mortar slurry, which is combined with chopped glassfibres that are fed simultaneously to the compressed air gun and sprayed onto the face mix. When a 4mm layer of backing mix is spread evenly across the face mix, it is rolled to remove any air voids before another 4mm layer is sprayed and compacted.

For this project the GRC mix was sprayed into plywood panel moulds lined with glass-reinforced plastic for a smooth finish and easy striking. First, the 4mm-thick facing coat, colour-matched to the Portland stone sample, was sprayed on. Then the backing coat of mortar with the glassfibre strands was sprayed in 4mm layers and rolled for compaction, to build up to the 16mm backing thickness. When the GRC panel was removed from the mould the hardened surface was given an acid-etched finish, and then supplied to Plus Wall on site to install under our supervision.

Typically the skin thickness of the panels was between 16mm and 20mm, making its self weight as much as 80 per cent lighter than a conventional precast concrete unit. Weight reduction of this magnitude offers substantial savings in transportation, handling and site erection costs.

The need for GRC cladding to be flexibly mounted on the supporting structure to accommodate thermal and moisture movements is important. Many of the problems associated with GRC have resulted from the lack of mobility in fixing design, from errors of installations or as a result of introducing some other, unintended, restraint to panel movement. Wherever possible, GRC panels should be designed as independent skins to allow maximum freedom to shape, curve and profile them. Good detailing of

panel size; reducing horizontal flat surface areas like window sills, which may collect surface water and create high moisture gradients in the panel; and avoiding panel shapes that wrap around a building corner, causing large thermal movements; will ensure a longer service life.

CONCRETE ELEGANCE//
03 SELF-COMPACTING CONCRETE

Self-Compacting Concrete
The City & County Museum, Lincoln

*Hugh Strange, Panter Hudspith Architects, and Mark Thomas,
Lafarge Ready Mixed Concrete*

Self-levelling, no-compaction concrete is arguably the panacea to achieving high-quality site-cast concrete finishes without the tears. It's not quite as simple as it sounds, and don't be fooled into believing that it can take the labour and cost out of concrete every time! However, when it works the results are truly stunning.

Architecture Outline

Hugh Strange, Panter Hudspith Architects

The project involved master planning the area surrounding the site, and the design of a new museum to house a substantial collection of archaeological and historical artefacts. The design of the museum creates connections through the site and improves links with the Usher Gallery and adjoining Temple Gardens. The external courtyard of the museum was designed to allow activities within the museum to spill out in the summer months, whilst also creating a new public space for Lincoln. The forms of the building fracture as they follow the contours up the hill and towards the Cathedral, opening up routes and views through the site. The external walls are angled planes of rough-faced limestone; the internal finishes are smooth, board-marked concrete.

Although we were designing a new building, it was important that it related to the medieval surroundings and to the topography of the site. We were interested in designing a modern building that could express something of the history of the city. When the Heritage Lottery Fund (HLF) were approached for stage one of the matched-funding application they asked the client to create a master plan for the surrounding Flaxengate area, so that the new building could be the catalyst for regeneration in the area. We then spend three useful months working on the master plan, really getting to know the city,

the pedestrian movements, the transport networks and local amenities. There was only one thing that unsettled us: it was when the client kept reminding us that they wanted the building to have a 'wow' factor. We felt it should not try to be a monumental statement, nor attempt to compete with the mighty Cathedral that was in view. We wished to design something that was much gentler, that sat well in the landscape, that did not shout out at you as you approached it but that nevertheless would be intriguing. The building is next to a park called Temple Gardens and on one side of it is the stone edifice of the Usher Gallery, built in the Palladian style, which houses the city's art collection. We thought the Usher Gallery in its park setting was very imposing and dominant, so we made the museum buildings flatter in scale and less imposing.

The major influence on the outward appearance of the building was the massive stone ramparts of the Bishop's Palace of Lincoln Cathedral that was set into the hillside. We felt there should be a certain massiveness about the museum buildings, so we conceived them as though they were being built out of five enormous blocks of stone. The first three mass together on the southern and lower end of the site; the next two blocks are slightly pulled apart. The building shapes can be read as hard landscape, which has cavities and openings for access and light.

Where there are doors and windows they cut into the stone. The building narrative is the arrangements of the windows, canopies, balustrades and doors and how they are inserted into the split limestone blocks.

The stonework of the façades is reminiscent of the stone beds in a quarry. The split limestone pieces are 100mm in width and 70mm in depth, which, when cut, maintains the rough surface of the stone you find in a quarry. They are bedded on mortar joints just like bricks, except they were only 5mm beds and the stones were cut into long lengths. The concrete internal structure came from the need to have high thermal mass in the building to conserve energy. Whether you are cooling it or heating it, the concrete acts as a thermal sink whatever the conditions. We also wanted the inside skin of the building to transform from a stone with fossils into something harder and rock-like. We wanted something that related to the stratification of the stones on the outside, so the board-marked concrete was ideal.

In terms of cost, the stonework was less expensive than the board-marked concrete walls. The redwood boards were planed smooth and had three different thicknesses. Even with such a smooth timber face, the self-compacting concrete picked up the subtle variations of the grain patterns and the knots. The benefits of self-compacting concrete were discussed at length with our structural engineers, Price and Myers. We were naturally concerned about the finish and getting the right people to supply it. We were advised that self-compacting would give an even colour, that it would have no blow holes on the surface and it would be the best material to cast the steep, variable pitches and twisted planes of the gallery roof; a normal concrete for the roof would have been impractical. The grey self-compacting mix we selected had a warm tone due to the limestone fillers. We spent a lot of time preparing layout drawings of the internal formed surfaces, matching the board marking to the 70mm coursing of the external stonework. The drawing would be sent to the concrete contractor, Northfieds, and their formwork specialist, DOKA. They would comment back about preferred tie-bolt locations, construction-joint details and panel sizes, and the working drawing would be amended until we were happy with the solution. It was very much a team effort. The self-compacting concrete gave a perfect 'porcelain' finish to the tongue-and-grooved board marked walls.

Self-Compacting Concrete

Mark Thomas, Lafarge Ready Mixed Concrete

Flowing self levelling, self-compacting concrete was supplied by our ready mixed plant in Lincoln. The self-compacting concrete which is branded 'Agilia' contains 400kg of Portland cement from Rugby's South Ferraby works, a nominal 10mm-graded limestone coarse aggregate; Trent Valley sand; and a percentage of fine limestone filler. The early trials showed the surface finish to have too many air pockets, an occurrence which was attributed to the angular-shaped limestone aggregates. This was changed to a smooth rounded single-size gravel, and the problem was solved. To obtain the self-compacting properties, the carefully blended material was mixed with a cement:aggregate ratio of 1:3, a water:cement ratio of around 0.6, and a suite of high-range water-reducing admixtures and surfactants to achieve the required cohesion and flow. No viscosity agent was used. The concrete achieved a flow of 500mm and the fluidity of the mix was maintained for 2 hours before it started to set. The concrete was placed by skip, using a flat hose attached to the discharge port. The hose was lowered down to the bottom of the formwork from one central point on the top of the wall panel. The concrete flowed down the hose to find its own level and fill the formwork, and the hose gradually rose

with the rising level of concrete. For the sloping roof, the concrete was placed through openings made in the top shutter near the base of the slope, and then from the top of the slope using a flat hose. The mix was ideal for vertical pours but was not suitable for flat slabs, where a power-floated finish was required. The formwork pressure can be much higher for this type of concrete, so the full hydrostatic head was assumed in the design of the formwork support system with a minimum movement permitted at tie-bolt positions. This ensured there was no grout loss, that the arrises and corners were sharp and day joints were neat. Properties of the hardened concrete do not differ significantly from those of ordinary concrete with a similar cement content. For compressive strength, the standard concrete-cube test is used. The extra cost of the higher cement content and special admixtures can be justified by savings in labour and by the blemish-free finish that can be achieved.

CONCRETE ELEGANCE//
04 RECYCLED CONCRETE INNOVATIONS

Recycled Concrete Innovations
the first step to a big idea

What can we do architecturally with waste glass from green wine bottles or crushed glass fines from TV monitors – apart from sprinkle it over the flowerbeds as decorative mulch and hope it will keep the snails away?
What about a flimsy geofabric for suppressing weeds or acting as a drainage filter, can it be used as formwork? The answer is yes – a new dimension in eco-friendly concrete expression that is novel and relatively cheap to use.

Recycled Formwork as Cladding
Tito Chaudhuri, Chaudhuri Architects

The idea to extend the ground floor area of my house into the garden started to germinate in 2002, a year after we had moved in to 22 Hoop Lane. I think it best to live in a house for a while before you make improvements. A ground floor extension at the back of the house was necessary in order to open out the cramped living room that was dominated by a 7ft-long dining table and an assortment of settees and armchairs. The concrete walls of the new extension were influenced by the work of architect Tadao Ando, and inspired by the fine concrete finishes achieved on the Aberdeen Lane House in Islington. That's how I got to know the concrete consultant David Bennett and became totally convinced that the walls had to be cast in concrete. I had briefly flirted with the notion of building the walls in lignacite blockwork because I did not have enough confidence in fair-faced concrete, and was mindful that the access to the house was along a narrow alleyway down the side of the neighbours' property. What you see at the end of the day with concrete is just the stick you are left holding at the end of the lollipop – what comes before that was a complete mystery to me! I had no comprehension of the labour involved, the detailing of tie-bolt holes and panel joints, having

to select formwork panels from a timber yard or of the number of weeks the builders would spend assembling the metal formwork-support system. (Nor how easily the driver of a huge ready-mix-concrete truck, manoeuvring itself towards the hopper of a concrete pump, can crack every pavement slab in his path in seconds and then deny it!) And then there was the bewildering array of pipes and hoses that snaked from the road to the back of the house to pump the concrete. I was gently eased into the chaos and upheaval of construction with words of encouragement and guidance from my concrete guru, as my living room was transformed into a builders' yard for cutting and lacquering sheets of birch ply and storing bags of nails, screws, plastic filler, release agent, sealant and all manner of building paraphernalia.

The 3.4m-long by 4.8m-wide by 2.8m-high internal space was designed to be very transparent, bringing the garden into the living room using a fully glazed end wall and a glazed roof spanning between the concrete walls. Cantifix supplied and erected all the glazing panels, and local builders Eldeco carried out the concrete work and other building jobs. The limestone flooring and the underfloor heating maintain a warm ambient temperature in the room even on the coldest days

– the concrete walls helping to retain the heat by their thermal mass.

What has been novel for me on this small yet significant project has been the reuse of all the birch ply formwork as cladding on the external face of the wall. The cladding mirrors the imprinted joints and layouts of the panels cast on the internal concrete walls. This not only saved money, but had environmental benefits by reducing site wastage and the creation of methane, which would have been generated by the plywood as it broke down in rubbish tips. I like to think that my property at 22 Hoop Lane has done its bit for mankind by reducing wastage positively and by reusing materials.

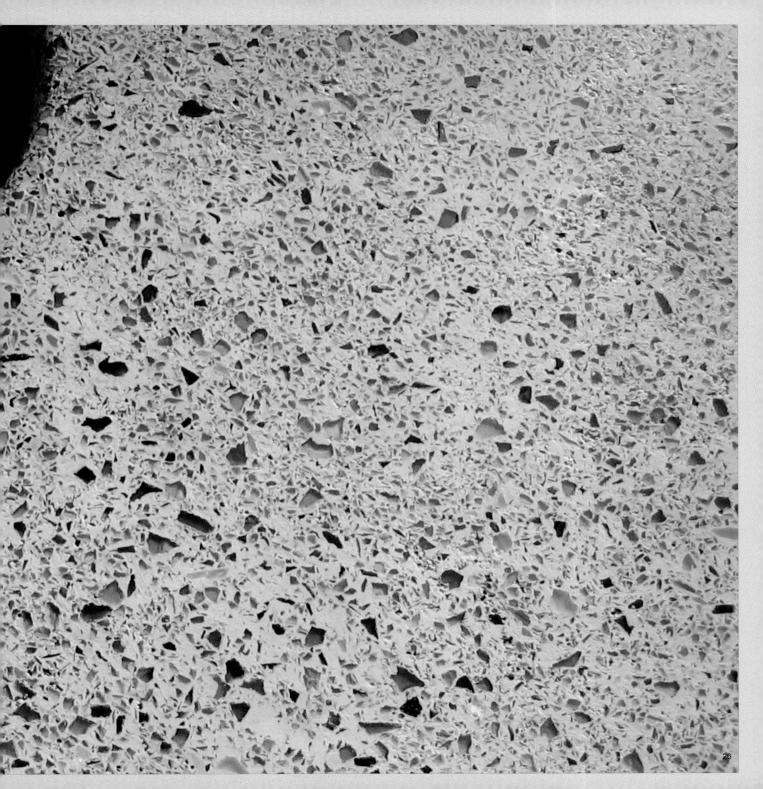

A Waste-Glass Concrete Worktop
Steve Bowkett, Tankard Bowkett Architects

The husband-and-wife team of architects, Jane Tankard and Steve Bowkett, have been involved in small bespoke residential and retail projects for a number of years, the largest of which was the conversion of a dilapidated warehouse in North Shoreditch in 1993 into artists' and architects homes'. They lived on one of the floors, which gave them 185 sq m (2,000 sq ft) of open-plan living space, and it was fine until their children arrived. It was a 'shock of the old' when they decided to move, now with two children in tow, to a three-storey house in Highgate which was full of small rooms. Their priority was to expand as much of the useable interior space between the party walls as possible. They converted the integral garage into a kitchen, made the staircase open-plan from ground floor to first floor and turned it 90° to create a bigger entrance lobby. The external glazed wall to the rear elevation was extended further out to the edge of the party walls, and converted the water-tank 'room on the roof ' into a habitable space. These many 'big-small' moves made a considerable impact on the overall house volume.

With a family of young children it meant that the open-plan spaces on each floor would have to be closed down into separate rooms using sliding and folding doors, so that the house has the flexibility to be configured into spatial arrangements of various sizes for sleep, play, study, entertainment and mealtimes. As architects, Tankard and Bowkett have always been interested in mixing both natural and synthetic materials in combinations – like concrete and limestone with rubber, perspex and glass. The paints they prefer are made from natural pigments, and lighting has been introduced to provide focal points. The showpiece of the house however, must surely be the hand-built kitchen, with its recycled perspex display screens (retrieved from a skip at South Bank University) and a stunning green-glass terrazzo concrete worktop.

The idea for the glass-aggregate worktop was suggested to the architects during a telephone conversation with David Bennett, the concrete consultant. Bennett proposed a concrete recipe that could be mixed on site using white cement and crushed TV-monitor glass, which was pale green and which would act as the fine aggregate, giving the concrete a pale green tint.
The 3–6mm-sized crushed green wine-bottle glass aggregates would be used for the 'terrazzo' effect. The recycled glass was supplied from Specialist Aggregates in Stafford, the white cement from a local builders' merchant, and the worry that it would not work was contributed by the client! A

small team of builders was employed to carry out the house improvements; the most able of them was delegated to work on the kitchen worktop frame and the concrete pour with Bowkett. The mould for the worktop was the frame and plinth of the kitchen cupboards below it: 18mm-thick water and boil-proof (WBP) plywood, which was overlain with polythene before the 50mm-thick semi-dry concrete terrazzo mix was placed, a bucket at a time. The trick was not to have the mix too wet, otherwise, on tamping it, too much fat would rise to the top and the aggregates would sink further down – thus making it very difficult to achieve the desired terrazzo effect.

The concrete was left to harden for a few weeks before a carborundum stone was used to polish the top few millimetres away, to reveal the shiny sparkling green glass 'jewels' beneath. Six coats of matt acrylic lacquer were more than ample protection against water ingress or staining. It is the first recycled-glass aggregate worktop to be built in situ, and hopefully the forerunner of many unique-yet-inexpensive, do-it-yourself worktop designs that any handyman can make.

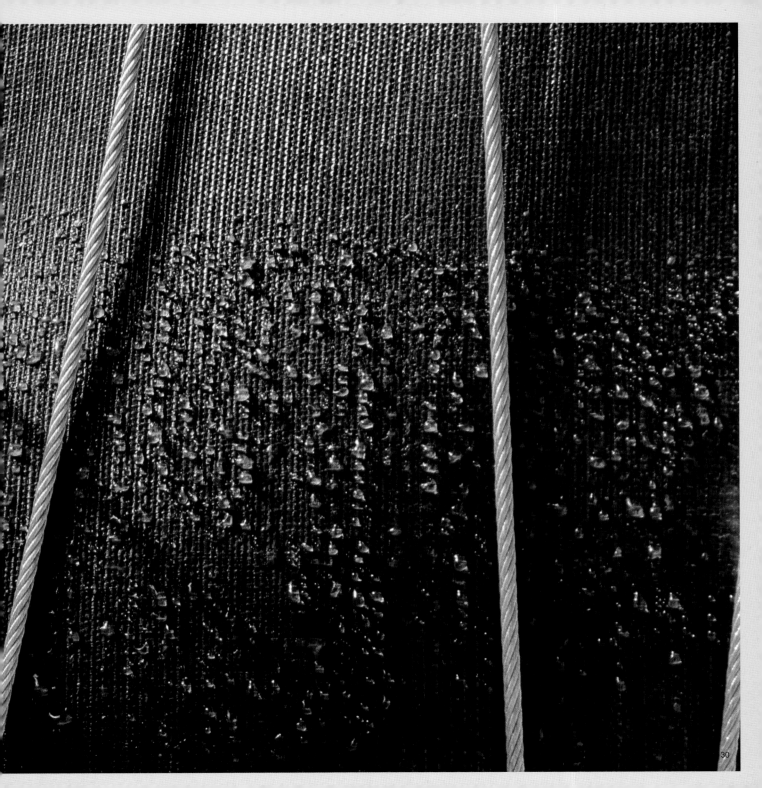

Fabric Forming Concrete – an Alternative to Plywood

Alan Chandler, University of East London

Fabric-formed concrete involves casting concrete with flexible geotextile fabric. By careful manipulation and stitching of this fabric, it is possible to produce complex free-form shapes that would not be possible using conventional plywood formwork. The permeability of the fabric reduces surface defects and improves the durability of the concrete. The surface finish follows the texture of the fabric and gives a cloth-like appearance.

A trial wall was built using a plywood frame and tension wires to confine the frame. A top board and base board of rigidly made timber joists were kept apart by a few adjustable metal props.
Wire strands, 4mm in diameter, were stretched between the top and bottom boards like a cat's cradle and tensioned against the props.
The fabric was then placed between the top and bottom boards and draped between the two vertical stop ends of timber like a stretched bag. The edges were pinned with battens to the timber framework to prevent the fabric bursting when the concrete was poured. The base board was shaped as a curving wave; the top broad was rectilinear to provide a changing geometry to the fabric. As the concrete was poured into the fabric bag, the tension in the wire was increased to retain the fabric wall while allowing the fabric to stretch.

At set intervals up the wall, steel rods with large wooden washers were pushed through the fabric just above concrete level to control the section thickness at those points. The wooden washers envelope the cross points of the tension wires to confine the concrete and create the 'mattress' effect you see on the concrete surface.

The concrete was placed quite slowly into the thin fabric mould without compaction. The mix was a conventional 1:2:4 (cement:sand:aggregate) mix by weight, but with more water added to compensate for the loss of water through the fabric. If the mix was too dry, the finish was poor. The wet concrete face in the fabric was given some hard slaps to drive the air and excess moisture out. It took about 30 minutes for the concrete to initially set, largely due to the resulting low water/concrete ratio and working indoors at about 20°C. The fabric was removed the next day and was washed. If it had not been badly torn by the tie rods it was reused, otherwise it was scrapped. All the framework, steel wire cables and props were reusable.

The coarse aggregate in the mix was a graded 6–20mm man-made material called 'MARC', derived from sintered sewage sludge and waste clay, which has been developed at UEL by Darrell

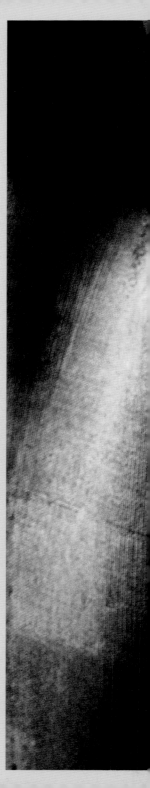

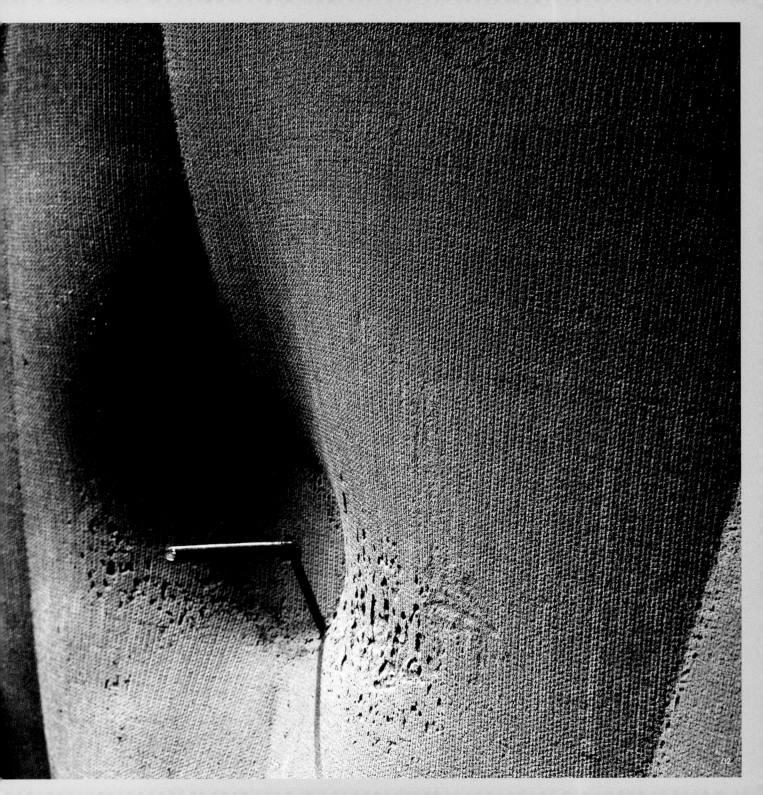

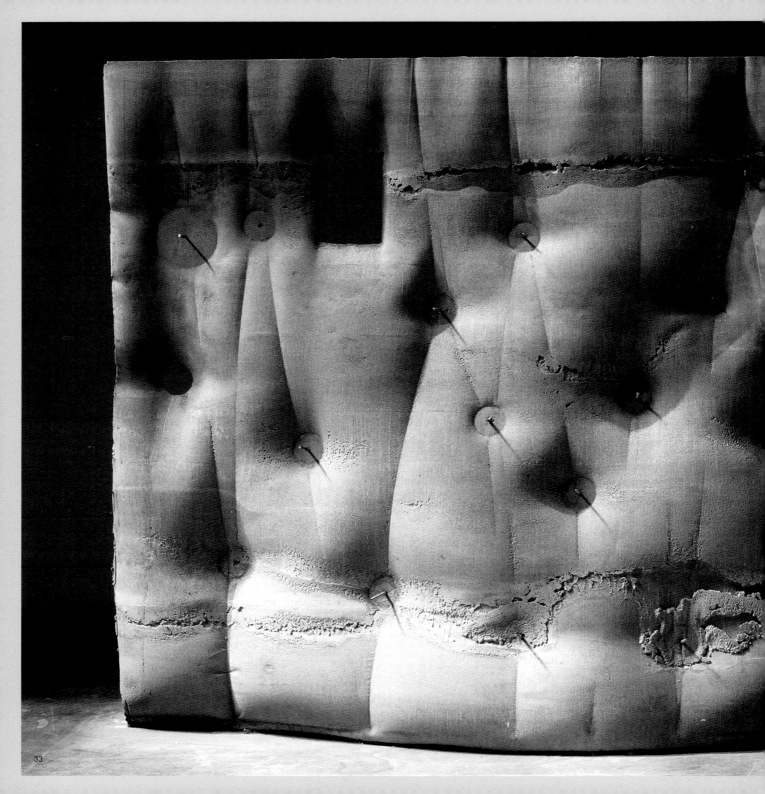

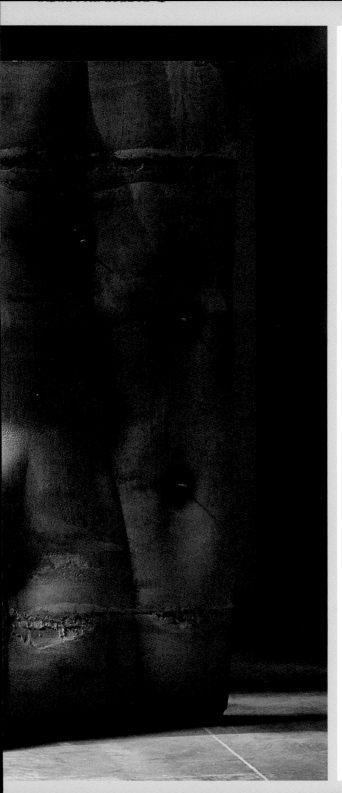

Newport, Director of Sustainability. There is a process plant at Tilbury where this material is being made. Three different sands were used to see the colour changes in the mix and the effect that this would have on surface appearance. The base mix used crushed MARC fines; the next layer, yellow Thames Valley sand; and the top, buff Leighton Buzzard sand. The colour variations when the grey concrete had fully carbonated were subtle. White cement might have shown more variation, and may be used on other trial walls.

This prototype wall has shown that it is possible to rethink in situ casting methods, using reusable fabric membranes instead of expensive plywood, and to significantly reduce site wastage and methane pollution.

CONCRETE ELEGANCE//
05 PRE-CAST COMPOSITE
INNOVATION

Precast Composite Innovation –
The Lean Cost Sandwich Panel
Anna Brunow, Brunow and Maunula Architects,
and Jorgen Sondermark, 3XNielsen Architects

The extraordinary use of space
for a low-cost residential building
in Finland uses mass produced
precast panels that have been
detailed with great care.
In Denmark a fresh approach
to head-office construction
derives its sophistication from
highly visible pigmented precast
sandwich panel construction,
commonly used for social
housing projects.

Saterinrinne Housing Development, Espoo, Helsinki
Anna Brunow, Brunow and Maunula Architects

There are two blocks in the housing scheme, one
of which sits on a large corner plot where the
council are planning to erect a footbridge. It was
not a good idea to have the views obstructed by
the footbridge. We therefore designed an open
space with a screen wall running into the corner,
while continuing the building line. The screen wall
encloses a small courtyard garden, and its frame
is made of steel with powder-coated metal infill
panels that mimic the shape of the external precast
panels and the window openings. Behind the
screen wall are planted some trees to emphasise
the open space.

Contractors in Helsinki seem to prefer to build
apartments with precast sandwich panels as they
are competitively priced, easy to erect, familiar to
site operatives and – most importantly – eliminates
the need for wet trades associated with brickwork.
The competition we had won, gave us the freedom
to design a façade that was different, rather than
a series of drab monolithic panels. We detailed a
single skin precast façade which was independent
of the internal load-bearing precast panel – it was
not strictly an all-in-one sandwich construction,
but it worked in the same way. The contractor
agreed to build this on condition that we made the
façade panels as big as possible and the same

size throughout! After making many sketches of panel shapes we decided on an L-shaped element that was just like a large jigsaw piece with straight sides. It could work one way and, if reversed or handed, could work the other way to create window openings. To break the regularity of the surface and to hide the joint lines we formed broad recesses on the panel surface, and these were coloured in a darker tone to pick out the irregular outline of the panels.

The precast single-skin panels were delivered with a plain grey untreated concrete finish, to which the contractor later applied a special silicate paint coat in accordance with our colour scheme. The flat surfaces of the panels were painted white and the recessed areas a pale green. Where we had staircases and lift cores, these were distinguished as towers that rise above the roof line. The core exteriors were painted yellow, red, green and blue according to their location. The flatness of the roof line was also broken up by the white precast balcony towers to the rear elevation, which stand proud of the building line. The pale blue-green of the rear elevation was the backdrop for these symbolic precast 'trees', whose trunks are framed by the white edges of the balcony slabs and supporting walls

SID Building, Arhus
Jorgan Sondermark, 3XNielsen Architects

We were very preoccupied in the early design
stages with the external appearance of the
building. Should it be glass curtain walling, powder-
coated aluminium cladding or a more integrated
structural approach – and one that related to the
surrounding landscape and responded to the
adjacent buildings? We decided on a black façade
to match the colour of the black metal-clad fascia
of the adjacent building. What we did not want to
construct was a building on the same lines as our
neighbour, which emphasised the horizontal. Ours
would accentuate the vertical.

Our choice was concrete because it was an organic
material derived from reconstituted stone, it can be
cast easily and moulded into curved and angled
shapes. Moreover, concrete and precast sandwich
panel construction were the most economical
choices.

In Denmark, sandwich-panel construction is
popular for residential buildings but not offices.
Together with our structural engineers, we looked
at the concept of sandwich-panel construction
to see how it could be assembled, and the units
stacked one on top of the other to form a wall
of colour with random window openings without
impairing structural integrity. Precast hollow core

38

floors, the roof and the precast staircase landings would span into this sandwich-panel wall to create one monolithic structure. The panels stack together, acting as a diaphragm wall, with the floors forming stabilising restraints. The load path from top to bottom flows around the window openings – even if the panels above and below have been stacked asymmetrically. This was a concept that we had been developing on other projects, but this was the first time it has been tried on such a scale. The inner load-bearing element of the sandwich panel, which was grey, was given a paint finish.

We planned the storey-high window openings based on four window-frame sizes, and then spread them in a random arrangement along each floor and over the entire elevation. What was interesting was that the price of the precast package became cheaper if we ordered only the solid unit sizes – the net size – with no window openings within them. Thus, we were able to make a saving of 35 per cent on the budgeted precast cost (with window openings)! These savings were spent on enhancing the window design, so that you could not tell the difference in frame thickness from those that opened and those that were fixed. This was quite an innovation.

One of the interesting phenomena that occur with black pigmented panels is that they will fade with time in a random way. The precast manufacturer warned us about it, and we also knew this from other panels we had designed with pigmented concrete. It was intriguing that the fade would not be the same across all panels, although they may have started off the same colour. As the building ages, the surface subtly changes tone year by year. The concrete, of course, remains perfectly weathertight and sound.

It has been confirmed that the New Museum of Liverpool in the UK is to be designed by competition winners 3XNeilsen Architects. Our design has been conceived as a building with inclined and elevated platforms that form an iconic sculptural structure. We hope there will be plenty of scope for precast and in situ concrete.

CONCRETE ELEGANCE//
06 ENGINEERED PRECAST ELEGANCE

Engineered Precast Elegance –
Refinement, Rigour and Simplicity
*Christian Hauvette, Christian Hauvette Architects, and
Linda Mattsson, White Architects*

The formal language of the architecture of the Katson Building in Stockholm is characterised by hard-driven structural demands of exposed precast concrete soffits, standardised columns and beams, neatly arranged mechanical and electrical systems and precise detailing. In the Paris project, the constraints of a triangular building plot made for an interesting architectural statement and a structural engineering challenge in precast concrete. The surface is exposed concrete – it's honest, self-supporting and robust.

9 Avenue René-Coty, Paris
Christian Hauvette, Christian Hauvette Architects

The most interesting feature of the building has been determined by the constraints of the triangular plot, onto which we had to shoehorn the building. It made for an interesting architectural statement and a structural engineering challenge. We like the natural grey of concrete as a surface because it looks like stone; it's honest and is the modern equivalent of the limestone construction of many old buildings in Paris. Concrete can be detailed and designed to respect the traditional style and rigour of the building lines set by these old stone buildings, so familiar along the Paris boulevards.

On the ground floor we have, in keeping with this tradition, slender circular columns inset from the transparent all-glass façade. Above this is a series of external beams and columns, forming a monumental grillage of Vierendeel frames that project forward of the ground floor line and rise up four storeys. The columns of this frame sit on a deep external precast beam at first floor level, which runs the length of the building. The columns and beams of the Vierendeel frames are all precast concrete and have the same width and surface finish. Within these frames a series of thin aluminium blades, like radiator grilles, comprise the mullions and transoms that project from the glass panels they support. The blades diffuse direct sunlight, helping to reduce solar gain and

internal temperature rise during the summer months.

The highest beam of the Vierendeel, at fourth-floor level, respects the cornice line of the existing buildings. We continued the top of the building to match the height of the double-storey mansard roofs of neighbouring buildings, creating an innovative filigree structure two storeys high that frames a glass curtain wall. The upper façade, which is set back from the Vierendeel line by 400mm, comprises a series of 8m-tall slender, tapering precast elements at 1m centres supporting a glass curtain wall. It seems very lightweight and visibly fragile compared with the dominant Vierendeel frames below it, which is the effect we wanted to create. The shape of the tapering columns symbolises, in many ways, the dramatic triangular plan of the site.

I like to find a kind of elementary grammar in my architecture, and a truth between the notion of object and event – and work on the idea of an architectural 'choreography' based on these relationships. It is possible, in my view, to conceive of fundamental relationships without stooping to catalogue sterility.

The Katson Building, Stockholm
Linda Mattsson, White Architects

The building has an uncomplicated external form
– it's a long narrow rectangular glass box with five
floors and a roof. The façade consists of a light metal
frame with glazing panels. On the roof is a single-
storey timber structure set back from the building
edge, and a terraced landscape. On the quay side,
built over the canal basin, is the main entrance to the
building.

The site was acquired by the practice in 1999
in competition with a developer who was also
interested in the plot. To avoid outbidding one
another the architects formed an agreement with
the developer, who agreed to buy back the building
once it was finished and to charge them a fixed
rent. The architects set the building budget at a
level not exceeding the rent they could afford to
pay. It's a unique solution, and one in which the
architect had control of the architecture, the internal
accommodation, the landscaping, the services and
the structure. It was important that they integrated as
a team within the practice and each discipline had a
proper function and reporting system.

Everything contributes to the structural or internal
fabric of the building. The detailing and design
of the building had to be precise and extremely
well coordinated. Poor detailing would show itself

and destroy the unity of the whole. There was, for example, no false ceiling to hide any unsightly service ducts, overhead lighting conduits or a poorly finished structural soffit.

The precast concrete structure is in effect, displayed in a glass showcase. The structural geometry was worked out carefully to make the joints and connections appear seamless, as though they had been poured in place. The double-T beam soffits were set flush with the primary beam soffits; the widths of the primary beams were made the same as those of the columns; and so on. The grey of the cement was the chosen colour for the precast, with a surface finish that was 'as struck' from the moulds. They did not want a white artificial concrete. It was not the intention to put the precast manufacturer under pressure to produce some dreamlike aesthetic finish, with acid washing or polishing. That was not central to the idea, and besides would have been a waste of money.

The thermal mass of the double-T precast floor was used as a heat sink and storage radiator. The concrete floor was cooled or heated by passing water pipes over the top of the precast slabs. Cool water from the canal (all free!) was circulated over the concrete to cool the floor and ceiling in the summer,

or heat was added to it during the winter to raise the water temperature. As the heavy concrete was slow to respond to changes in the water temperature, the indoor climate only varied from 22°C to a maximum of 26°C, which was quite acceptable. The cold air draughts created by convection currents off the external glass during freezing winter months was abated by hot-water convectors fitted near to them.

The **Concrete** Centre

The Concrete Centre
Riverside House
4 Meadows Business Park
Station Approach, Blackwater
Camberley, Surrey GU17 9AB

t: 01276 606800

www.concretecentre.com

For free help and advice on the design,
use and performance of concrete, please call
The Concrete Centre's national helpline
on 0700 4 500 500 or 0700 4 CONCRETE

All 'Concrete Elegance' events are free of charge
and take place in the Building Centre in the
evenings. To attend any event, or to find out about
current and future programmes, please contact
The Concrete Centre or the Building Centre Trust.